THE BUILD
OF A
WINNING TEAM

Enhancing Group Performance

MW00641624

By Tim L. Holman
PO Box 353
North Hampton, Ohio 45349
(937) 964-15341

Front Cover
Dolores Bowers

Copyright © 1998
Tim L. Holman
PO Box 353
North Hampton, Ohio 45349

All rights reserved.

Library of Congress Catalog Card Number: 98-92980

ISBN: 1-57502-825-5

Scripture taken from the HOLY BIBLE,
NEW INTERNATIONAL VERSION
NIV . Copyright © 1973, 1978, 1984
by International Bible Society.
Used by permission of Zondervan Publishing House.
All rights reserved.

Printed in the USA by

3212 East Highway 30 • Kearney, NE 68847 • 1-800-650-7888

TABLE OF CONTENTS

As iron sharpens iron,
so man sharpens another.
Proverbs 27:17

CHAPTER ONE

An Overview
of the
Building Blocks

● ●

*Strive for excellence in
all that you do.*

Coaching requires you to bring the team from where it is to where it wants to be.

THE BUILDING BLOCKS

Small businesses, large corporations, churches, and families are finding it difficult to do all that needs to be done. This is why teams can be so important. Simply put, a group can accomplish more. In Ecclesiastes 4:9 the author states, "Two are better than one, because they have a good return for the work." In Mark 6:7 Jesus knew the benefits of a team. That is why he sent the disciples out in teams of two.

Now many will agree that putting a team together is easy. Keeping the team working in a cohesive manner is the difficult task. *The Building Blocks Of a Winning Team* is a proven method for keeping teams on track.

The Building Blocks are made up of two sections. First, there is the foundation consisting of two elements. Then there is the structure section, which is made up of nine elements. I will cover each section in detail.

THE FOUNDATION

The foundation consists of creating and communicating a vision and setting goals. The foundation provides a focus for the team. This is a key element since the lack of focus is the most common cause of team burnout. Teams simply can't function unless all the members are focused and moving in the right direction.

The vision is a look into the future of what can be. In other words, what specifically does the team need to accomplish and, if the team accomplishes the team goals, what will the end results look like.

Let's look at it from another angle. Walt Disney

had a vision. The vision was Disney World in Florida. He was able to communicate that vision so well that everyone could see it. Now many people say that it was a shame that Walt Disney died five years before Disney World was completed. They say that he was never able to see the amusement park, but, Walt Disney did see it in it's completed form. In fact, he saw it long before anyone else. Now that's focus.

Walt was able to communicate the team vision in a very vivid way. All team members would see the reality of Disney World. The team leader cannot lead a team where he or she cannot see. This is why the vision is so important.

Jesus knew the importance of focus. That is why He told His disciples to not worry about food and clothing when He sent them out. He wanted them to focus on their mission. Once this type of focus is established, people will move together toward that focus.

Team goals are also important in getting a team to function effectively. Goals need to be **S**pecific, **M**easurable, **A**chievable, **R**ealistic, and **T**ime dimensional. Goals provide the *how* in reaching the vision.

I have found that whenever possible, team members should help establish these goals. This provides them with a sense of ownership, and when there is ownership, people tend to work harder to accomplish the goals.

You can see what the lack of focus can do. Just look at certain athletic teams or corporate teams. Show me a team that is not functioning effectively and I'll show you a team that has lost its focus. Establish a vision and set goals to reach that vision. Keep that focus in front of the team and there is no limit to what a group of people can do. Add to this the power of prayer and you might even be able to tear down the walls of Jericho! In Genesis 11:6 the Lord said if the people have one purpose, nothing will be impossible for them.

THE STRUCTURE
Now that we have established a focus, let's move on to the structure of The Building Blocks.

BUILDING BLOCK #1- Build Trust
Whenever a group of people come together, it is not unusual to see personal agendas develop. When this occurs, the trust level tends to be non-existent.

Trust is the cornerstone of the *Building Blocks.* Without trust, people will not communicate in an open way and relationships cannot be formed.

A cohesive team is dependent on a high trust relationship, with everyone looking out for each others interest. Jesus wanted people to understand this when he said, "Nobody should seek his own good, but the good of others". (I Cor.10:24.)

If team members are constantly asking themselves if they can trust each other, the team will become paralyzed and unable to advance forward.

Talking is probably the best way to increase trust. Sitting down in an informal setting and talking with other members of the team will go a long way in building trust. Since understanding is the key to trust, talking will help each team member build trust.

As you begin to form your teams, you may want to do a few sessions on building trust early in the process. If the trust level is already high, you will find little time is needed on this *Building Block.*

Each team member must be committed to the success of the team. They must support each other and help each other grow and develop. If you concentrate on helping others succeed, you are letting everyone know that you are there for the right reason and you don't have a personal agenda.

An important aspect of trust is the personal integrity of each member of the team. Trust will extend to the limit of truth, and no further. If a team member is holding something back or not totally honest about their intentions or activities, the trust of the entire team is affected.

Team members must do what they say they will do. All team members are dependent on each other. Therefore, members must live up to the expectations of the team.

Remember, it is the success of team performance, not individual performance that is important. Lou Holtz, the successful football coach, uses this philosophy: "Do what's right; Do the best you can; Treat others the way you want to be treated." That's good advice from someone who is a very successful builder of winning teams.

BUILDING BLOCK #2 - Maintain a Positive Attitude

How's your attitude today? What type of attitude will you bring to the team? Well, to be successful, a winning team needs a positive attitude.

So, what is an attitude? An attitude is an inward feeling expressed by an individuals behavior. I can think of few things that are as contagious as an attitude. So if one individual comes to the team with a bad attitude, it will spread like a wildfire.

As it is stated in Ephesians 4:23, team members should bring a new, refreshing attitude to the team. The attitude should be positive, looking for and concentrating on the positive aspects of the objectives of the team. This is difficult for some people to do. They are used to concentrating on the past and the negative. This attitude will prevent the team from moving forward. Sure, there will be problems, but every problem is an opportunity and in every adversity there is some good. The key is to seek out and focus on the good things.

Attitude is a choice. When you get out of bed in the morning, you make a choice. Do I want to be in a good mood or a bad mood? The choice is totally yours. Ask yourself what attitude would Jesus want you to have? Read Philippians 2:5.

I was doing a seminar in Columbus, Ohio a few years ago and we were discussing attitudes. I had just explained how important a positive attitude is to the team. A young man in the back of the room stood up with a somewhat angry "attitude" and said, "You don't know what I've been through. I deserve to have a bad attitude." Now that's an attitude! Well, I stopped and asked him one question. "Has the bad attitude helped you deal with your problems?" He thought for a moment and said, "No." Then he sat down. You see, we all are dealing with a lot of issues in our lives, but we can approach any situation with more success if we have a positive attitude.

Now, let's look at this from a team standpoint. Every team will have problems. The question is, can the team turn those problems into opportunities? Every team will run into adversity, but can the team find good in that adversity? The high performance team can and will seek out the good.

Team members must focus on the positive and approach the task at hand with a *can do attitude.* Isn't this what Jesus expects? He doesn't want us to go about our work with a "Woe is me" attitude. Jesus gives us hope. What better reason to have a positive attitude. Through Jesus, the team can accomplish anything. What better reason to be positive!

BUILDING BLOCK #3 - Allow Mistakes

Whenever I talk about allowing mistakes, many people think I'm saying it's ok to perform poorly. But nothing could be further from the truth. There is a big difference between the two.

First, poor performance means the same mistakes are repeated over and over. Allowing mistakes means that when someone tries something new, it's ok if they make a mistake. That is with one condition. We must learn from the mistake and take action to prevent the same mistake from occurring again. This will affect how we will approach the same task the next time. In essence, there is no such thing as a mistake, only lessons in education. Constantly learning from our mistake helps us grow.

Think about it. Did Jesus allow mistakes? How many times did the disciples make mistakes? How did Jesus respond? He was patient and understanding. Proverbs 19:11 says, "a man's wisdom gives him patience." The disciples grew and learned from their mistakes. That's what made them strong team members in spreading the word.

Many people will resist team activity because they have a fear of failure. However if these people know that they are allowed to make mistakes and the team is there to support them, the fear of failure is reduced. Take their fear away and team members will become cohesive.

This means that we must keep a positive attitude towards mistakes. Talk to other team members about mistakes. Get their input. Educate the entire team about the lessons learned. Now everyone can learn and the entire team begins supporting each other. As a result, attitudes improve and trust builds. Proverbs 27:23 says, "Know well the conditions of your flocks, and give attention to your herds."

BUILDING BLOCK #4 - Educate
The word "educate" as used in this *building block* does not refer to a college degree. Rather, it is promoting group dynamics. Many groups don't work well together. This may be the result of people who have never functioned within a team. Most people are used to working by themselves. When placed in a situation where they have to work together with other team members, they are sometimes uncomfortable. This is not to say they don't want to work with others. Instead, they just don't know how to function effectively in a team atmosphere. Thus the team leader must teach the elements of team work. Proverbs 10:14 states that "Wise men store up knowledge." Wise team members do the same.

So just what should team members be taught? Well, the *building blocks* that we have been describing are a good start. Bring your team members together and discuss each *building block.* Ask how the elements of each can be accomplished. Which elements do they feel comfortable with and which do they need to improve upon?

Group dynamics, conflict resolution, the decision making process, and communications are just a few examples of the skills that should be taught to every team member. However every team member must understand that in no way do these things take priority over prayer.

Prayer is the basis of members working together. Ask Reggie White of the Green Bay Packers how important prayer is to the team. Reggie leads frequent prayer groups prior to games. Maybe

13

ou're a little skeptical, but you can't argue with the success of the Super Bowl champs.

Teach the team the importance of prayer. No matter how well you're functioning as a team, don't forget to pray. Pray for God's will to be revealed. Pray for other team members. Pray for good decision making. Pray before conflicts arise. Pray for direction and, when these prayers are answered, give praise to God for the answers!

Your team members must understand that God is a member of the team and He provides the path for the team. Psalm 32:8 reads, "God will instruct and counsel us." Matthew 7:7-12 says that we should; "Ask...seek...knock."

BUILDING BLOCK #5 - Communicate

Communicate, communicate, communicate. I repeat this three times to show the importance of this *building block.* It should also be noted that "communicate" is the very center of *building blocks.* Without good communications, teams cannot and will not function effectively. Genesis 11:1-9 says "A common language helped the builder of the tower of Babel."

Communication is based on three parts. Each part needs to be considered very carefully. First, there is the non-verbal communication, better known as body language. This makes up 50% of our communication. Think for a minute about the body language you have witnessed. If you are talking to someone and the entire time you are talking, the person is looking out the window, what message is being sent? What if someone keeps looking at their watch? What does a frown mean? Or perhaps folded arms across the chest? What about eye contact? Each of these acts distort communication.

The second part of communication is the tone of voice. The tone of a persons voice makes up 35% of communication.You can say the same words to an individual but, by changing the tone of your voice, you can alter the meaning behind those words. Take for example, "I want to see you in my office!" Now try saying these words by changing your tone. Can you see how the meaning of the words could change? Team members must be very aware as to how they say phrases when they attempt to communicate.

The third part of communication is words. Words make up only 15% of communication. It seems strange that words represent such a small percentage of importance in communicating, but it's true.

Consider the many words in our vocabulary that sound the same but have entirely different meanings. A few examples are to, too and two. Or how about the words buy, by and bye? With this in mind, you should choose your words carefully when communicating. Don't be placed in a position in which you are misunderstood. Let's look at another example to help emphasize this point. From the list below indicate the percentage of time that each word represents.

Always _____   Often _____
Sometimes _____   Never _____
Frequently _____   Seldom _____

When you compare the answers, you will see that many different interpretations are found for the same word. How does this affect communications? If one person thinks "sometimes" represents 20% of the time and another person thinks it means 10% of the time, problems will arise.

Communication does not take place until the receiver receives the message as the sender intended it. The only way this can be accomplished is for the sender to work with the receiver to make sure that understanding has taken place. Questions must be asked and clarification made. In Matthew 13:51, Jesus made sure that the audience understood exactly what He said.

BUILDING BLOCK #6 - Think Win-Win

Our society has moved quickly to a win-lose mentality. We think, how can I win? Many people could care less *how* they win but, in a team environment, we must stay focused on the importance of win-win.

Win-win is not a compromise. A compromise means someone is going to give up something. In a win-win situation both parties win. However , this is not always as easy as it sounds. When we encounter difficult situations, we sometimes think we know best. Therefore, we take the bull by the horns and try to take action on our own. This is usually a mistake. The Lord knows what's best in every situation and, if He is left out of that situation, it will always be a win-lose.

Try this exercise with two people. Place a piece of tape on the floor. Now have one person stand on each side of the tape facing each other. Explain that the goal is for each person to convince the other to step to the other side of the tape. No force is allowed. In most cases the two will negotiate for up to 20 minutes trying to get the other person to step over the tape to their side. I have performed this exercise with people in many areas of the country and the result is almost always the same. A stand off. Most people want to win, and sometimes we want to win so badly that we will become stubborn and hard to deal with.

The point is we need to stay focused on God's

will and then the team will always come up with a win-win solution.

BUILDING BLOCK #7 - Have Fun
This building block is very simple. God wants us to have fun and enjoy life. If a team is working together to do the work of the Lord, what could be more fun? Habakkuk 3:18 says, "I will be joyful in God my savior."

Team activity, by nature, is fun. When a group of people come together and work for a common cause, there is a sense of enjoyment felt. When this common cause is centered around the Lord's work, even more enjoyment can be experienced.

All team members will bring different skills and diverse talents to the team. As you learn to capitalize on these different skills and talents, you will see the group come together and enjoy each other. 1 Timothy 6:18, "God, who richly provides us with everything for our enjoyment."

BUILDING BLOCK #8 - Keep Score
Score keeping is a vital part of a team. It motivates and keeps the team on track. If no one keeps score, the team has no way of knowing what progress they are making.

Let's look at a basketball game. The score is 56 to 46. The team with 46 points is motivated to do what? Score more and catch up, right? The team with 56 points is motivated to stay ahead. Now let's take the score board down. I just made 12 points. Who cares? Since no one is keeping score, the game has no meaning. How do we know what progress is being made? Who's winning? What does the team need to do to win?

It's important to remember that scores are *not*

kept on individuals. Individual score keeping will stimulate competition. You may be asking,"What's wrong with competition?" The answer is, nothing, as long as individual team members are not competing against each other. This is a team, remember? The only competition you want to see is the team as a whole competing against the team goals. Therefore you will want to focus your score keeping in this area. Matthew 7:35 (paraphrased) says, "Why look for a speck in your team mate's eye when there is a plank in your own eye?"

BUILDING BLOCK #9 - Recognize and Reward
Recognition and rewards will help keep the team motivated, but we must look at the significant difference between the two.

Recognition is usually visible and not tangible. Saying"Thank You! You did a good job!" or a written "thank you" in the newsletter or on the bulletin board are all examples of recognition.

A thank you note sent to a team member's home is one of the best recognition systems that I have found. Be innovative and see what other ways you recognize team performance.

Rewards, on the other hand, are tangible. Things like plaques, gift certificates or certificates of recognition are a few examples of rewards. Matthew 25:21 tells us that the Master recognizes good work.

Those are *The Building Blocks* . Concentrate on each one until your team has them perfected. You will accomplish more in less time and you can have fun in the process. Many organizations have spent thousands of dollars trying to perfect the team concept. You can have a cohesive team by just following these simple steps. They have been tried and proven time and time again with great success. So, form a team and keep them focused, and you will see great things happen in the name of the Lord.

CHAPTER TWO

What's So Important About Teams?

● ●

So we rebuild the wall till all of it reached half it's height, for the people worked with all their hearts.

Nehemiah 4:6

" It's easy to get the players.
Getting them to play together,
that's the hard part."
Casey Stingle

ADVANTAGES OF TEAMS

1. Teams promote efficiency.

2. Teams promote quality.

3. Teams promote innovation.

4. Teams build relationships.

5. Teams are cost effective.

6. Team give more power to employees.

7. Teams reduce errors.

8. Teams work smarter.

9. Teams increase flexibility.

10. Team increase quality of work life.

11. Teams reduce waste.

12. Teams assure continuity.

13. Teams accomplish more.

14. Teams continue to improve.

"Two are better than one... There is better return for the labor of a group. There is strength in numbers.

Ecclesiastes 4:9-12

WHAT'S SO IMPORTANT ABOUT TEAMS?

1. Team building is a process, not a program.

2. Teams expose feelings.

3. Teams provide rapid decision making.

4. Teams break down barriers.

5. Teams increase dedication and commitment.

6. Teams increase the fun in the workplace.

The quality of a team is in direct proportion to the commitment to excellence.

CHAPTER THREE

THE STAGES OF
TEAM BUILDING

●●●●●●●●●●●●●●●●●●●●●●●●●●●●●●●

**Look towards the interest
of others.**

Phillipians 2:4

Never doubt that a small group of thoughtful, committed people can change the world. Indeed, it is the only thing that ever has.

STAGE ONE - FORMING

1. No common vision or purpose.

2. Training is initiated.

3. Roles of team members are not defined.

4. People don't know each other.

5. Team concept is introduced.

6. There is no interdependence.

7. Some resistance may be encountered.

The forming stage will vary in time depending on size and maturity of the organization.

*"The price of greatness
is responsibility."*
Winston Churchill

THE QUESTIONS EVERY TEAM MEMBER WILL ASK?

1. Why am I here?

2. What is my role?

3. What is our purpose?

4. Do you care about me?

5. Can I trust other team members?

6. Are we all seeking excellence?

These questions should be answered in the Forming Stage.

We win and we lose as a team.

STAGE TWO - STORMING
(This is normal)

1. Individual and organizational Strengths, Weaknesses, Opportunities, and Threats are established within the group.

2. Personal agendas are placed on the table and discussed with all members.

3. Reservations and feelings are discussed.

4. Differences in personalities are revealed and discussed.

5. The past is discussed and put to rest.

6. There are more "ME" attitudes than "I" attitudes during this stage.

7. There is no "Interdependence" in this stage.

8. Turf battles will occur.

This stage can be painful but it's necessary.

Working together for a common purpose....That's teamwork!

STAGE THREE - NORMING

1. Vision and goals become more visible.

2. Roles of members are clarified.

3. There is more understanding and caring within the team.

4. The purpose of the team is clear.

5. Team members expectations are understood.

6. Less resistance is seen.

7. Team concept can be seen in some areas of the organization.

8. Team performance is beginning to improve.

9. "We" attitudes are now more important than the "Me" attitude.

The Norming Stage confirms....This thing can work!

Teamwork.........
Divides the task and doubles
the success.

STAGE FOUR - PERFORMING

1. Vision and goals are well defined and shared.

2. Members are *"FOCUSED"*.

3. Members carry out their roles.

4. Team expectations are high.

5. Consistent cooperation is seen.

6. "We" attitude is promoted by all members.

7. Team concept is seen consistently throughout the organization.

8. Group behavior is mostly positive.

The team has arrived. But, left alone everything will revert back to the way it was.

Therefore everyone who hears these words of mine and puts them into practice is like a a wise man who builds his house on the rock.

Matthew 7:24

CHAPTER FOUR

THE FOUNDATION

• •

"Where there is no vision the people will perish."
Proverbs 29:18

"The future belongs to those who believe in the beauty of their dreams."

Eleanor Roosevelt

THE BUILDING BLOCKS OF A
WINNING TEAM

CREATE THE VISION	**DEVELOP TEAM GOALS**

THE
FOUNDATION

*A positive thought
is the seed
of positive results.*

CREATE THE VISION

Every organization needs a sense of direction. Without it, the members become confused and tend to do "their own thing." This can lead to fragmentation, low morale and low productivity. Vision is seeing what may be. Vision brings the future into today's activity.

Think of your organization and answer the following questions:

- Where is the organization going?

- If the organization could be anything what would it be?

- What is the ideal organization?

- What should the organization look like?

- What would we need to do to be more successful as an organization?

- How do we become a better organization?

> Vision:
> Is the driving force of the organization.

*Success is a journey,
not a destination.*

"Vision...it reaches beyond the thing that is, into the conception of what can be. Imagination gives you the picture. Vision gives you the impulse to make the picture your own."

Robert Collier

Continue to answer the following questions:

- What is the most important aspect of the organization?

- What gives the organization meaning?

- What does the future hold for the organization?

SWOT ANALYSIS

Strengths _____

Weakness _____

Opportunities _____

Threats _____

Teamwork is the fuel that allows common people to attain uncommon results.

OUR TEAM'S VISION..

_____

_____

_____

Remember.....
You cannot lead where
you cannot see.

Tim Holman

*Let your eyes look straight
ahead, fix your
gaze directly before you.*

Proverbs 4:25

```
                    ┌──────────────────────┐
                    │                      │╲
                    │   TEAM GOALS         │ │
                    │                      │ │
                    └──────────────────────┘╱
```

HOW TO ACCOMPLISH
"TEAM GOALS"

1. Set Smart Goals - All goals must be:

    Specific
    Measurable
    Achievable
    Realistic
    Time Dimension

2. Determine the objectives (Tasks)
    • How will the goal be reached?
    • What tasks need to be accomplished?

3. Make the goals visible
    • Write the goals down.
    • Display on wall or bulletin board.

4. Give specific assignments to team members.
    • Delegate the tasks.

5. Review progress
    • Identify the barriers.
    • Keep score.

6. Evaluate
    • What is and is not working?
      (Modify as needed)

I press on toward the goal to win the prize for which God has called me heavenward in Christ Jesus.

Philippians 3:14

ADDITIONAL GOAL CONSIDERATIONS

1. Identify any barriers that may have to be overcome.

2. Make sure the goal provides action.

3. Get input from all team members.

4. Make the goal visible to all team members.

5. Review the goals frequently.

6. Give specific assignments based on objectives.

7. Recognize accomplishments.

TEAMWORK....
Success is achieved when all members work together.

CHAPTER FIVE

THE STRUCTURE

• •

**Teamwork is the fuel
that allows common
people to attain
uncommon results.**

Remember....
Possibilities are the only things
that are truly limitless.

THE BUILDING BLOCKS OF A
WINNING TEAM

HAVE FUN	**KEEP SCORE**	**RECOGNIZE and REWARD**
EDUCATE	**COMMUNICATE**	**THINK WIN-WIN**
BUILD TRUST	**POSITIVE ATTITUDE**	**ALLOW MISTAKES**

THE
STRUCTURE

*If a man has made a promise,
he must not break his word.*
Numbers 30:2

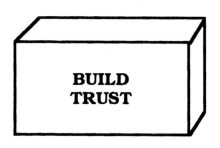

BUILD TRUST

1. Support each other.

2. Communicate openly.

3. Do not talk behind each other's back.

4. Do what you say you will do.

5. Keep the success of the team in mind.

6. Praise and recognize good team work.

7. Show you care about other team members.

8. Do that which is right.

9. Seek excellence.

10. Treat others the way you wish to be treated.

If you have not been trustworthy with someone else's property, who will give you property of your own.

Luke 16:12

BUILD TRUST

Questions to discuss with your team.

1. Think of someone you trust. Now list all the characteristics of that individual.

2. Why should people trust you?

3. Do you feel other team members trust you? Why?

4. Describe in detail how you will build trust within the team.

5. Define, "do that which is right."

Simply let your yes be yes and your no be no.
Matthew 5:37

Create in me a pure heart, O God, and renew a steadfast spirit within me.

Psalm 51:10

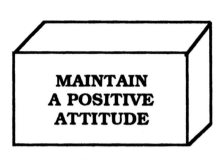

MAINTAIN A POSITIVE ATTITUDE

1. Attitude is an inward feeling expressed by your behavior.

2. Your attitude will influence others, make sure you are a positive influence.

3. Attitude will determine your success rate.

4. You have a choice.....You can choose to have a attitude or a bad attitude. Choose the good.

5. Have a caring attitude toward other team members.

6. Your self image will influence your attitude.

7. Remember.....There is opportunity in every adversity.

8. Think positive, take positive action, be a positive example.

9. Don't let negative people influence you.

10. Develop a "CAN DO ATTITUDE."

You were taught, with regard to your former way of life, to put off your old self, which is being corrupted by it's deceitful desires; to be made new in attitude of your minds; and to put on a new self, created to be like God in true righteousness and holiness.

Ephesians 4:22-24

MAINTAIN A POSITIVE ATTITUDE

Questions to discuss with your team.

1. How is your attitude today?
   Excellent   Good   SoSo   Bad
   Why?

2. Do you do things for the *RIGHT* reasons?

3. Do you *REGARD* others as more important than yourself?

4. How do you view your childhood days?
   Loving   Secure   Stable   Bad

5. Success is _____.

6. How do you view your personal life?
   Positive   Negative

7. How do you view your job?
   Positive   Negative

8. Which is more important, that which happens to me or how I respond to that which happens? Why?

9. What we sow is what we reap?
   True   False

10. How often do you experience negative thinking?
    Frequently   Seldom   Rarely

Therefore, since Christ suffered in his body, arm yourselves also with the same attitude.

1 Peter 4:1

The last of the human freedoms is to choose one's attitude in any given set of circumstances.

Victor Frankl

11. When do you allow other people to influence negative thinking?

12. How does negative thinking blow things out of proportion?

13. Why is negative thinking contagious?

14. How will you avoid negative thinking?

The air currents of life jolt us out of line and try to keep us from achieving our goals. Unexpected weather can change our direction and strategy. We must adjust our thinking continually so we can live right.

John Maxwell

"Let us not lose heart in doing good, for in due time we shall reap if we do not grow weary."
Galatians 6:9

Change the following *negative* words into positive words.

Try

Can't

Won't

If

Maybe

Doubt

Impossible

Blame

Keep

Argue

Criticize

Tear down

Problem

Adversity

Failure

Discourage

When I am secure in Christ, I can afford to take a risk in my life. Only the insecure cannot afford failure. The secure can be honest about themselves. They can admit failure. They are able to seek help and try again. They can change.

John Maxwell

ALLOW MISTAKES

1. Analyze mistakes and learn from them.

2. Think of mistakes as"Lessons in Education".

3. Correct your mistakes and strive to do better.

4. Keep a positive attitude towards mistakes.

5. Talk to other team members.....get their input.

6. Support those that make mistakes. Help them prevent future mistakes.

7. Remember that mistakes help you grow.

8. When mistakes occur, educate other team members so they can learn too.

9. Never look at a mistake as being a failure.

10. Remember.... Thomas Edison tried 5000 elements before he invented the light bulb.

Wisdom comes more from living than from studying.

ALLOW
MISTAKES

Questions to discuss with your team.

1. When you try something new do you approach it
with:
- Fear
- Confidence
- Reservation
- Resistance

Why ?

2. How do you feel when other people make
mistakes that affect you ?
- Angry
- Willing to help
- Judgmental
- Resistant

Why ?

3. You grow as an individual by _____.
- Taking risk
- Learning from mistakes
- Watching other make mistakes
- Staying in your comfort zone

4. How do you feel when you make a mistake ?
- Angry
- Stupid
- Positive
- Negative

It's not whether you get knocked down. It's whether you get up again.

Vince Lombardi

Failure is only the opportunity to more intelligently begin again.
Henry Ford

5. How do you expect others to respond to your mistakes?
   - With understanding
   - Critical
   - Willing to help
   - Anger

6. How easy is it for you to take a risk?
   - Very easy
   - Somewhat easy
   - Seldom easy
   - Never easy

Why?

7. What is the biggest mistake you ever made?

_____
   - What did you learn?
   - Would you be willing to try again?
   - What would you change?

8. When is it easy to make a mistake?

9. What makes it difficult?

10. Why is risk taking important for the team?

Failure is only seen when we fail to learn from our mistakes.

*How much better to get
wisdom than gold,
to choose understanding
rather than silver.*
Proverbs 16:16

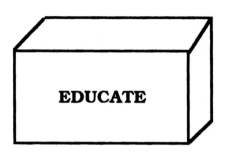

EDUCATE

1. Assure team members have strong technical skills needed to perform their job.

2. Provide ongoing training.

3. Seek excellence.

4. Teach support skills:
   Group dynamics, communications, problem solving, decision making, quality tools, conflict management, attitude, meeting skills.

5. Identify the roles of each team member.

6. Set expectations for team participation.

7. Determine individual growth needs.

8. Select magazine articles that would benefit the team. Assign articles to team members to read. Have team members review article at next meeting to allow all members to learn.

9. Expect excellence from all team members.

10. Become a learning organization.

He who listens to a life-giving rebuke will be at home among the wise.

Proverbs 15:31

EDUCATE

Questions to discuss with your team.

1. What role will you play for the team?

2. How will this role help the team succeed?

3. In what areas does the organization need to improve performance?

4. What training is needed to improve the performance of the organization?

5. What continuing will the team need?

6. What expertise do we have within the team?

7. What support skills will the team need?

8. How will we obtain the training?

9. When will training take place?

10. What is the ideal length of the training sessions?

He who walketh with wise men shall be wise...
Proverbs 13:20

We must be wiser today than yesterday.

Tim Holman

THE CROSS TRAINING PROCESS

Trainer   1. Show what the end result should be.

Trainer   2. Explain what determines the quality.

Trainer   3. Visualize and verbally walk through the process that is being taught.

Student   4. Have student review what you have covered with them.

Trainer   5. Do the actual step by step process.

Trainer   6. Review necessary steps and solicit questions from the student.

Student   7. Have student perform the actual actual process while trainer observes.

Trainer   8. Review the students' work while concentrating on the good.

Trainer/   9. Determine areas that are weak and
Student   need improvement.

Trainer/   10. Repeat steps 1 through 9 as needed.
Student

Note: This process can be used at home for young members of the family or in the workplace to help individuals grow and develop.

We always seem to place more emphasis on what we don't want people to do than what we want them to do.

Tim Holman

THE PROBLEM SOLVING MODEL

1. Identify the problem

2. Identify potential causes

3. Identify most probable cause

4. Identify the alternative solutions

5. Predict good and bad outcomes

6. Select the best solution

7. Develop a plan of action

8. Implement the plan

9. Evaluate the plan

10. Repeat any steps as needed

Remember , problems are opportunities in disguise.

"The tongue that brings healing is a tree of life, but a deceitful tongue crushes the spirit."
Proverbs 15:4

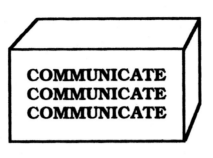

1. Communication consists of:
   50% Non-Verbal
   35% Tone of Voice
   15% Words

2. Share information and data.

3. Listen with empathy.

4. Keep communication lines open and two way.

5. Avoid distracting environment and interruptions.

6. Remember....effective communication depends on two parties, the sender and the receiver.

7. Communication only occurs when the receiver receives the message as the sender intended.

8. Understand the meaning of words as they are presented.

9. Don't assume you know the meaning behind a conversation.

10. Good communication depends on cooperation between the sender and the receiver.

*"Wise people will listen
and learn more."*
Proverbs 1:5

COMMUNICATE
COMMUNICATE
COMMUNICATE

Questions to discuss with your team.

1. What barriers exist with our communications?

2. How can we break down those barriers?

3. When we communicate do we understand each other?

4. How do emotions interfere with communications?

5. Why is team communications important?

6. Review the following list of communication barriers. How can we eliminate them?

Words	Organizational Structure
People	Perceptions
Authority	Noise
Influence	Lack of Understanding

***Pay close attention and
gain understanding.***
Proverbs 4:1

I believe that you can get everything in life you want if you just help enough other people get what they want.

Zig Ziglar

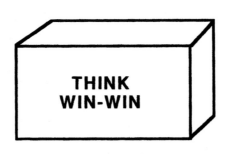

THINK
WIN-WIN

1. Win - Win is not a compromise.

2. Both parties win.

3. Compromise means someone will lose
   something during negotiations.

4. In a Win - Win situation a new approach is
   developed and adopted.

5. Win - Win helps build synergy.

6. Win -Win is a "we" attitude.

7. Win - Win promotes interdependence.

8. Win - Win promotes goodwill.

Seek first to serve others.

*The master recognized
good works.*
Matthew 25:21

THINK
WIN-WIN

Questions to discuss with your team.

1. Describe a win-win situation in which you have been involved.

2. Win-Win is a _____.
   - Me Attitude
   - They Attitude
   - We Attitude

3. Win-Win is more _____.
   - Independent in nature
   - Interdependent in nature

4. Make a list of obstacles that keep you from reaching a Win-Win solution.

   _____
   _____
   _____
   _____
   _____

5. How can you promote Win-Win in your team?

   _____
   _____
   _____
   _____

Remember: If you don't care who gets the credit the team can accomplish anything.

Have fun and create great things.

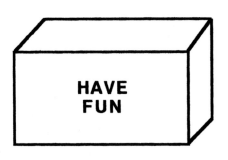

HAVE FUN

1. Your work needs to be enjoyable.

2. When your work is fun other areas of your life are enhanced.

3. Team work will add fun to the job.

4. Help others have fun.

5. Develop an environment that encourages fun.

6. Have a desire to accomplish more.

7. Eliminate frustrations within the team.

8. Enjoy the relationships of other team members.

Adopt a positive attitude towards your work.

A man can do nothing better than to eat and drink and find satisfaction in his work.
Ecclesiastes 3:24

HAVE
FUN

Questions to discuss with your team.

1. What do you like most about your job?

_____

_____

2. Is your job fun........
    • Most of the time?
    • Sometimes?
    • Seldom?
    • Never?

3. How can you bring more fun to the workplace?

_____

_____

4. How work fun change your approach to work?

_____

_____

5. What can team members do to make the
   workplace fun?

_____

_____

6. What attitude do you bring to the team?

_____

_____

7. Why is it important to have fun at work?

_____

_____

A happy person is not a person in a certain set of circumstances, but rather a person with a certain set of attitudes.

Hugh Downs

Happiness....it lies in the joy of achievement, in the thrill of creative effort.
Franklin D. Roosevelt

8. How does fun improve the team process?
_____
_____

9. Do you look forward to your work day?
Why ?   Why Not?
_____
_____

10. How does happiness or fun relate to success?
_____
_____

11. How does fun relate to satisfaction?
_____
_____

12. Are you using your full potential? Why?
_____
_____

There is joy in work...........
There is no happiness except
in the realization that we have
accomplished something.
Henry Ford

If no one was keeping score.....
who would play the game?
Tim Holman

KEEP SCORE

1. Develop a Score Board.

2. Decide what standards will be scored.

3. Use team goals as part of the scoring process.

4. Develop simple charts.

5. Make score keeping visible.

6. Involve team members in the scoring process.

7. Keeping score gives focus to the work.

8. Build rewards and recognition programs into good scores and performance.

9. Competition should be towards the team goals not between team members.

10. Score boards are used to encourage and to motivate........not to point fingers or ridicule.

People need feedback for growth and development.

SCORE BOARDS

Teach team members to:

1. Keep score

2. Gather data

3. Analyze data

4. Relate data to team performance

KEEP
SCORE

Questions to discuss with your team.

1. How do we know if the team is reaching its goal? _____

   _____

2. How do we make our progress visible to all team members? _____

   _____

3. What indicates team success? _____

   _____

4. Can we measure this success? _____

   _____

5. Who should keep the score? _____

   _____

6. Why should we avoid keeping score on individual team members? _____

   _____

7. How does score keeping help motivate team members? _____

   _____

8. In what way does the data we collect relate to team performance? _____

   _____

Do not withhold good from those who deserve it, when it is in your power to act.

Proverbs 3:27

**RECOGNIZE
AND
REWARD**

1. Recognize good teamwork.

2. Recognize success.

3. Recognize good scores.

4. Recognize team goal accomplishment.

5. Simple rewards mean a lot.

6. Praise good performance.

7. Base rewards on performance.

8. Change rewards frequently.

9. Rewards and recognition must be meaningful.

10. Rewards do not have to be expensive for them to have meaning.

11. A sincere "thank you" is very valuable.........the key word is *Sincere.*

12. Rewards and recognition should meet the needs of the people.

***The master recognized
good works.***
Matthew 25:21

REWARDS
AND
RECOGNITION

The rules of developing a system:

1. Develop the criteria
   - What is the goal or standard?

2. Keep Score
   - Gather the data.
   - Focus on the positive.

3. Make it visible
   - Hold a rally.
   - Use news letters
   - Use scoreboards.

4. Make it meaningful
   - Promote a sense of accomplishment.

5. Be innovative
   - Look for new ways to recognize and reward the people.

6. Change the reward from time to time
   - Keep it a surprise.

7. Remember little things mean a lot
   - Send thank you cards to members' home address.

8. Link rewards to performance
   - What behavior do you want?

Look to the interest of others.
Philippians 2:4

RECOGNIZE
AND
REWARD

Questions to discuss with your team.

1. What motivates you?

2. Is it possible to motivate others?

3. When should the team be recognized?

4. How can you reward other team members?

5. What is the difference between rewards
   and recognition?

6. What kind of team performance do we want?

7. What types of rewards are meaningful?

8. How can we make recognition and rewards
   more visible?

MOTIVATION.....Is based on meeting the needs of the people!

***A patient man has
great understanding.***
Proverbs 14:29

CHAPTER SIX

THE COACHING MODEL

• •

INSPIRE

TEACH

REDIRECT

*For a lack of guidance
a nation falls.*
Proverbs 11:14

THE COACHING MODEL

Try filling in the blanks without looking at the answers on the next page

1. Set _____.

2. Train _____ and _____ _____.

3. Build _____.

4. Be _____ and _____ with everyone.

5. Encourage the people to take additional _____.

6. Monitor _____ and _____.

7. Keep _____.

8. Give _____.

9. Keep _____ lines open.

10. Make _____ as needed.

How good it is when brothers live in unity.
Psalm 133:1

Obstacles are those frightful things you see when you take your eyes off your goal.

THE COACHING MODEL

ANSWERS

---

1. *Goals*

2. *Technical and Support Skills*

3. *Trust*

4. *Firm and fair*

5. *Risk*

6. *Progress and Performance*

7. *Score*

8. *Feedback*

9. *Communication*

10. *Adjustments*

First Seek the counsel
of the Lord.
1 Kings 22:5

THE COACHES RESPONSIBILITY TO THE TEAM

1. Communications

2. Provide a Focus

3. Motivate

4. Give feedback

5. Promote Growth and Development

6. Teach

7. Results

8. Provide Resources

A wise man keeps himself under self-control.
Proverbs 29:11

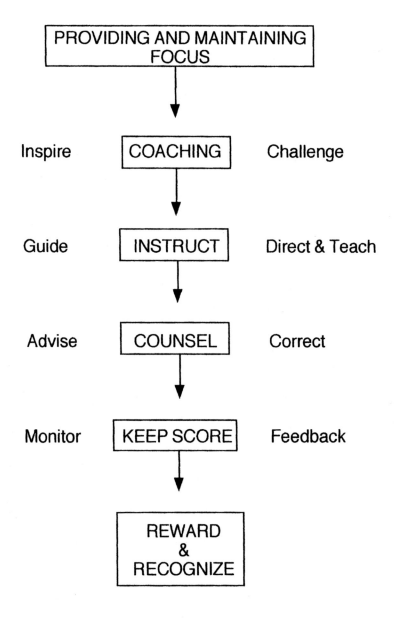

THE COACHING CONCEPT

PROVIDING AND MAINTAINING FOCUS

Inspire   COACHING   Challenge

Guide   INSTRUCT   Direct & Teach

Advise   COUNSEL   Correct

Monitor   KEEP SCORE   Feedback

REWARD & RECOGNIZE

Nobody should seek his own good, but the good of others.
1 Corinthians 10:24

QUESTIONS EVERY COACH SHOULD ASK

1. Have I taught the people the skills they need to perform the task?

2. Have I provided the people with the time needed to perform the task?

3. Have I provided the people with the resources needed to perform the task?

Coaching.........
It's an integral part of leading.
Tim Holman

THREE REASONS WHY TEAMS FAIL TO SUCCEED

1. Lack of Focus

2. Personal Agendas

3. Lack of Caring

*"If you don't grow,
you go!*
Ken Blanchard

SEVEN EXPECTATIONS OF A TEAM MEMBER

1. Have a winning Attitude.

2. Treat others the way you wish to be treated.

3. Capitalize on Diversity.

4. Seek Excellence.

5. Do that which is right.

6. Stay Focused.

7. Participate.

Our objective ought to be to have a good army rather than a large one.
George Washington

Remember.........

Team building is a process. It has a beginning but there is no end. It continues to evolve, becoming better and better with time. If you begin today, the team should be more cohesive tomorrow.

Team building requires patience. There will be "ups" and "downs" but, as the team matures, the "downs" will be less frequent.

Teams require a constant "shot in the arm." Left alone, the team will dissolve and everything will revert back to the way it was before team building.

Keep the team focused. Motivate them and provide them with continuous education.

Contrary to many peoples belief, God does have a place in the workplace and the family. Only when He was eliminated did we start experiencing problems of great magnitude in all areas of our society.

If you continue to do what you have always done, you'll always be what you've always been.

Good luck and may God bless.

ABOUT THE AUTHOR

As a speaker and seminar leader, Tim has conducted programs throughout the United States. He specializes in helping individuals and organizations maximize their potential.

Tim graduated with honors from Ottawa University in Kansas. He has an extensive background in health care management, the fire service and organizational development.

As a member of the National Speakers Association, Tim is frequently requested to speak at conferences and retreats across the country. He is known for presenting highly unique and motivating programs that give practical solutions to today's hectic and demanding world.

Tim has written numerous articles for national journals and also published the *Ten Commandments of Highly Successful Leaders.* (Morris Publishing)

Tim resides in West Central Ohio with his wife Becky and their three daughters.

For more information about books or seminars please contact:

Tim Holman
PO Box 353
North Hampton, Ohio 45349
(937) 964-1534

NOTES

NOTES

NOTES

NOTES

NOTES

NOTES

NOTES

NOTES

NOTES

NOTES

NOTES